WHAT ARE MINERALS?

CORONA BREZINA

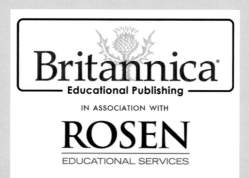

Britannica®
Educational Publishing

IN ASSOCIATION WITH

ROSEN
EDUCATIONAL SERVICES

Published in 2019 by Britannica Educational Publishing (a trademark of Encyclopædia Britannica, Inc.) in association with The Rosen Publishing Group, Inc.
29 East 21st Street, New York, NY 10010

Distributed exclusively by Rosen Publishing.
To see additional Britannica Educational Publishing titles, go to rosenpublishing.com.

First Edition

Britannica Educational Publishing
J.E. Luebering: Executive Director, Core Editorial
Mary Rose McCudden: Editor, Britannica Student Encyclopedia

Rosen Publishing
Kathy Kuhtz Campbell: Senior Editor
Nelson Sá: Art Director
Nicole Russo-Duca: Series Designer and Book Layout
Cindy Reiman: Photography Manager
Nicole DiMella: Photo Researcher

Library of Congress Cataloging-in-Publication Data

Names: Brezina, Corona, author.
Title: What are minerals? / Corona Brezina.
Description: New York: Britannica Educational Publishing, in Association with Rosen Educational Services, 2019. | Series: Let's find out! Good health | Audience: Grades 1–4. | Includes bibliographical references and index.
Identifiers: LCCN 2017050389| ISBN 9781538303023 (library bound) | ISBN 9781538303030 (pbk.) | ISBN 9781538303047 (6 pack)
Subjects: LCSH: Minerals in nutrition—Juvenile literature. | Nutrition—Juvenile literature.
Classification: LCC QP533 .B74 2019 | DDC 613.2/85—dc23
LC record available at https://lccn.loc.gov/2017050389

Manufactured in the United States of America

Photo credits: Cover, back cover, pp. 1, 12, 17, interior pages background bitt24/Shutterstock.com; p. 4 Richard Griffin/Shutterstock.com; p. 5 Tatyana Vyc/Shutterstock.com; p. 6 DAJ/Getty Images; p. 7 SW Productions/Stockbyte/Thinkstock; p. 8 Roman Tiraspolsky/Shutterstock.com; p. 9 U.S. Food and Drug Administration; p. 10 © International Osteoporosis Foundation; p. 11 Tatsiana Tsyhanova/Shutterstock.com; p. 13 Lerner Vadim/Shutterstock.com; p. 14 Catalin Petolea/Shutterstock.com; p. 15 Catalina M/Shutterstock.com; p. 16 Susumu Nishinaga/Science Photo Library/Getty Images; p. 18 Encyclopædia Britannica, Inc.; p. 19 Artur Begel/Shutterstock.com; p. 20 Kateryna Kon/Shutterstock.com; p. 21 Blend Images/Shutterstock.com; p. 22 Nicole DiMella; p. 23 Carlos Osorio/Toronto Star/Getty Images; p. 24 Karan Bunjean/Shutterstock.com; p. 25 Chubykin Arkady/Shutterstock.com; p. 26 JGI/Tom Grill/Blend Images/Getty Images; p. 27 Harry Hu/Shutterstock.com; p. 28 Timof/Shutterstock.com; p. 29 Nina Dermawan/Moment Mobile/Getty Images.

CONTENTS

Introducing Minerals

Minerals are a kind of nutrient. Nutrients are things that a body needs in order to grow and stay healthy. They are an important part of the human diet. Certain daily amounts of dietary minerals are required for strong bones, muscles, and other parts of the body.

Minerals are inorganic substances, meaning that they come from rocks and other nonliving things. Plants take in minerals from the soil. Animals obtain minerals by eating plants and the milk, eggs, and meat of plant-eating animals.

Nutritionists are experts who give advice on how food

Plants grow and thrive by taking in minerals from the soil through their roots.

Eating a banana at breakfast is nutritious. Bananas contain the mineral potassium.

affects health. They sort minerals into two categories: macrominerals and trace minerals.

Macrominerals are also called major minerals. People need to consume more than 100 milligrams, or 3.5 ounces, of these minerals every day. Calcium, magnesium, phosphorus, sulfur, sodium, potassium, and chloride are macrominerals.

The trace minerals include iron, zinc, copper, manganese, iodine, selenium, fluoride, molybdenum, and chromium. People need smaller amounts of each trace mineral—less than 100 mg daily.

THINK ABOUT IT

Why is it important to get enough minerals in your diet when you are young and your body is growing?

Minerals and the Human Body

Most nutrients are metabolized by the body. They provide energy for the body's activities. Minerals, on the other hand, are not metabolized. They do not provide energy.

Milk is a good source of calcium, which the body uses to build strong bones.

Minerals such as magnesium are required for the body to build strong bones and for muscles to work smoothly.

Minerals perform different functions. They provide structure—for example, calcium makes bones hard. They also do specific jobs—for example, iron helps blood to carry oxygen around the body. Some minerals are particles with an electric charge. They help to regulate processes in the body.

Most minerals are involved in a variety of functions. For instance, magnesium helps the muscles work. It also helps to build bones and to control blood sugar levels.

Minerals make up about 4 to 6 percent of a person's body weight. About one half of this amount is calcium. About one quarter is phosphorus, which is also found in bones and teeth. Trace minerals do not add much to body weight.

MINERALS AND DIET

Humans get dietary minerals from both plant and animal food sources. Amounts of minerals in a food can vary. A plant's mineral content, for example, can depend on growing conditions. Cooking methods can reduce the minerals in food. Some foods, such as salt and cereal, have minerals added to them to make them more nutritious. These are called fortified foods.

The body must absorb dietary minerals to use them. Various factors affect how well the body absorbs minerals. In general, minerals are better absorbed from animal foods than from plant foods. Also, minerals can interact with

COMPARE AND CONTRAST

Check the food labels of some of your favorite foods. What minerals do they contain?

each other. This means that the presence of one mineral can decrease the absorption of another. A person's physical condition can affect absorption as well.

Many packaged foods have labels that show nutritional information, including amounts of minerals. These amounts include minerals that are naturally in the food and minerals that were added through fortification.

New Label

Nutrition Facts

1. 8 servings per container
   Serving size 2/3 cup (55g)

2. **Amount per serving**
   Calories **230**

   % Daily Value*

3. **Total Fat** 8g — 10%
   Saturated Fat 1g — 5%
   Trans Fat 0g
   Cholesterol 0mg — 0%
   Sodium 160mg — 7%
   Total Carbohydrate 37g — 13%
   Dietary Fiber 4g — 14%
   Total Sugars 12g

4. Includes 10g Added Sugars — 20%
   Protein 3g

5. Vitamin D 2mcg — 10%
   Calcium 200mg — 15%
   Iron 8mg — 45%
   Potassium 235mg — 6%

6. * The % Daily Value (DV) tells you how much a nutrient in a serving of food contributes to a daily diet. 2,000 calories a day is used for general nutrition advice.

data shows that it is difficult to meet nutrient needs while staying within calorie limits if you consume more than 10 percent of your total daily calories from added sugar.

5. Nutrients

The lists of nutrients that are required or permitted on the label have been updated. Vitamin D and potassium are now required on the label because Americans do not always get the recommended amounts. Vitamins A and C are no longer required since deficiencies of these vitamins are rare today. The actual amount (in milligrams or micrograms) in addition to the %DV must be listed for vitamin D, calcium, iron, and potassium.

The daily values for nutrients have also been updated based on newer scientific evidence. The daily values are reference amounts of nutrients to consume or not to exceed and are used to calculate the %DV.

6. Footnote

The footnote at the bottom of the label has changed to better explain the meaning of %DV. The %DV helps you understand the nutrition information in the context of a total daily diet.

Nutrition facts labels give information about food, including the mineral content. This information helps people to choose the healthiest options.

CALCIUM

Calcium is essential for strong bones and teeth. People require calcium at every stage of their lives. Kids need calcium to build strong bones. Adults need calcium to prevent bones from becoming weak. People who do not get enough calcium are at a high risk of having osteoporosis later in life.

These pictures show a normal bone (*left*) compared to a bone with osteoporosis.

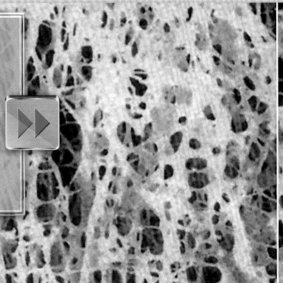
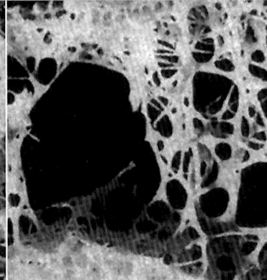

Calcium performs other important functions in the body, too. It helps muscles to contract, or tighten, when they move. It also plays a role in sending messages through the nervous system.

Many people, especially tweens and teenagers, do not get enough calcium in their diet. Milk and dairy products are great sources of calcium. Other foods high in calcium include fish (especially fish like sardines, where the bones are eaten) and green leafy vegetables. Some foods, such as orange juice and cereal, are fortified with calcium.

Milk · Soymilk · Enriched Breads & Grains · Almonds · Soybeans · CALCIUM · CALCIUM RICH FOODS · Green Peas · Cheese · Broccoli · Cabbage · Sardines · Oranges

Eating a variety of calcium-rich foods helps to build healthy bones and teeth.

Magnesium, Phosphorus, and Sulfur

The mineral magnesium is important in regulating many processes in the body. Some of these include muscle and nerve function, regulation of blood sugar levels, and the heartbeat. Magnesium also helps to build bones and to produce protein and energy. Good sources of magnesium include green leafy vegetables, legumes (including beans, peas, and lentils), nuts, and whole grains.

Phosphorus is needed to build bones and teeth. It is also involved in other functions, such as the growth and repair of cells in the body.

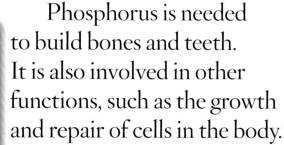

Almonds, spinach, beans, bananas, and avocados are some sources of magnesium.

Magnesium is found in chlorophyll, the substance that makes plants green. Many plant foods are good sources of magnesium. Sulfur is found in protein, which makes up muscles. Can you name foods you eat that probably contain sulfur?

The mineral sulfur is part of some of the building blocks that make up cells. It also plays a role in cellular respiration, which is the process that cells go through to get energy from nutrients.

Phosphorus and sulfur are found in many foods. Sunflower seeds, Romano cheese, and salmon contain phosphorus. Cauliflower and other members of the cabbage family are rich in sulfur. Most people do not have to seek out specific foods containing these minerals.

Cauliflower and cabbage contain sulfur and other nutrients that are vital to good health.

Sodium, Potassium, and Chloride

The minerals sodium, potassium, and chloride act as electrolytes in the body. They work together to control the movement of

Vocabulary

Electrolytes are ions, or particles with an electric charge. They help to regulate processes performed by the cells of the body.

While being physically active, people should drink water to maintain a fluid balance in the body.

Chicken and sweet potatoes are rich in potassium.

fluids in and out of cells, including the blood. Drinking plenty of water is important in order to keep a balance of electrolytes and to avoid dehydration.

Each of these minerals has other important functions, too. For example, sodium and potassium play roles in the function of muscle and nerve cells. Chloride, found in stomach acid, aids in digestion.

Sodium and chloride make up table salt. Most people do not have to worry about getting the required amount. Potassium is found in meat, poultry, some fish, certain vegetables (especially sweet potatoes and squash), certain fruits (especially bananas), nuts, and dairy products.

IRON

Iron is one of the trace minerals. People require it in much smaller amounts than macrominerals. Still, iron is a very important dietary mineral.

Most iron in the body is contained in red blood cells. The body uses iron to build a substance called hemoglobin in the blood. Hemoglobin carries oxygen to all the cells in the body. Oxygen and hemoglobin combine to give blood its red color. The body's cells use the oxygen to do their jobs. Iron is also responsible for other functions, such as supporting metabolism and keeping cells healthy.

There are two forms of dietary iron. Heme iron is more easily used by the body. It is found in meat, poultry, and

In each red blood cell, an iron-rich substance called hemoglobin carries oxygen.

Eating plenty of foods with heme and non-heme iron helps the body's red blood cells to work properly.

seafood. Non-heme iron is found in plants. Sources of non-heme iron include nuts, legumes such as lentils and beans, dried fruits, grains, and vegetables. Combining iron-rich foods with sources of vitamin C helps the body to absorb iron.

Think About It

Vegetarians do not eat meat or poultry. Why should they take special care to include enough iron in their diets?

OTHER TRACE MINERALS

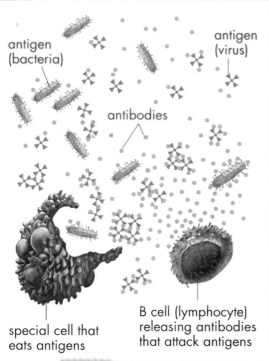

antigen (bacteria)

antigen (virus)

antibodies

special cell that eats antigens

B cell (lymphocyte) releasing antibodies that attack antigens

Some trace minerals—zinc, copper, iodine, manganese, selenium, molybdenum, and chromium—may not sound like familiar nutrients. But they are all important in keeping the body healthy.

The mineral zinc is the second most plentiful trace mineral in the body, behind iron. It plays an important role in the immune system and in the senses of smell and taste. Children need zinc for healthy growth and development.

Special cells that eat harmful bacteria and viruses (called antigens) are a part of natural immunity, the protection given by the immune system.

VOCABULARY
The **immune system** protects the body from germs and other outside substances that can cause disease.

Shellfish is low in fat and highly nutritious. It contains protein as well as several key vitamins and minerals, including copper.

Good sources of zinc include oysters, meat (such as lamb and beef), poultry, beans, and nuts.

Copper helps to produce red blood cells. It also supports nerve cells and the immune system. Copper is found in oysters and other shellfish, whole grains, liver, and dark leafy green vegetables.

Iodine is important for the function of an organ called the thyroid gland. The thyroid gland uses iodine to produce a substance called thyroxine. Thyroxine helps the body's cells to function normally. Iodine occurs in plants and animals from the sea, such as shellfish and seaweed. Dairy products also contain iodine. Table salt often is fortified with iodine as well.

The thyroid gland is a butterfly-shaped organ located at the base of the neck. The thyroid uses iodine to make the substance thyroxine.

The mineral manganese plays a role in the action of many enzymes, which are proteins that perform specific jobs. Manganese also is important in the reproductive system. Dietary sources of manganese include nuts, seeds, whole grains, legumes, green leafy vegetables, and tea.

Selenium helps the body to make enzymes. Some of these enzymes protect cells from being damaged. Food sources include Brazil nuts, seafood (especially tuna, halibut, and sardines), ham, beef liver, whole grains, and dairy products.

Other trace minerals in the body include molybdenum and chromium. They are present in small amounts.

Fluoride added to drinking water and toothpaste helps to keep cavities from forming in the teeth.

Molybdenum helps certain enzymes to do their jobs. Chromium helps to regulate blood sugar. Some food sources for molybdenum are legumes, grains, and nuts. Chromium is found in broccoli and grape juice.

Fluoride is sometimes considered a dietary trace mineral, but it is not required for health. Fluoride is added to toothpaste and water supplies to prevent tooth decay.

THINK ABOUT IT

Have you noticed that green leafy vegetables contain many important minerals? What is your favorite way to eat your greens?

NOT ENOUGH MINERALS

People who do not take in minerals for a long period of time can develop disorders. The disorders depend on which mineral is deficient, or missing from the diet. For example, a deficiency of calcium can lead to osteoporosis, especially in older adults.

How do people know whether they are getting enough minerals? A value called the recommended dietary allowance (RDA) is the daily amount of a nutrient

The nutrition facts label for a box of cereal shows that three quarters of a cup (twenty-nine grams) fulfills part of the daily recommended dietary allowances for calcium, iron, and magnesium.

A vegetarian meal can provide plenty of minerals if it includes a variety of nutritious whole grains, fruits, and vegetables.

that a person needs. This value is not the same for everyone. It depends on factors such as gender and age. Food labels list the average RDA for every mineral that is included in a serving.

Certain factors may increase the likelihood of mineral deficiency. People who restrict their diets, such as vegetarians, may have trouble getting enough dietary minerals. (Vegetarians can get the minerals they need by choosing the right variety of foods.) Some medical

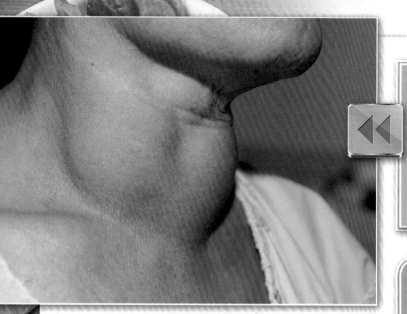

A lack of iodine in the diet can cause a condition called goiter, a swelling of the thyroid gland.

conditions can affect digestion or cause a patient to require more minerals. Children, pregnant women, and older adults may be at a higher risk of mineral deficiency.

The most common mineral deficiency is a lack of iron, which can cause anemia. For children, iron deficiency can harm growth, development, and learning ability.

An iodine deficiency can cause a condition called goiter. This is a swelling of the thyroid gland in the neck.

Some people like to squeeze lemon over fish. Try new flavor combinations in order to include a broader range of healthy foods in your diet.

It is possible for people to develop deficiencies in zinc, magnesium, or other dietary minerals, but these cases are uncommon. Still, it is a good idea to eat a balanced diet that includes a variety of healthy foods. An overall nutritious diet contains the right levels of minerals for most people. It can be fun to try preparing new foods that are full of minerals and other nutrients.

COMPARE AND CONTRAST

In the past, diseases caused by iodine deficiency were common. Today, they are very rare. Can you explain why?

MINERAL SUPPLEMENTS

A healthy diet usually provides adequate minerals. Yet, many people take supplements to make sure that they get enough minerals. Supplements can contain a single mineral or several minerals. Supplements made up of many minerals and vitamins are called multivitamins. Supplements can treat or prevent mineral deficiencies. Still, it is better to get minerals from whole foods, when possible, because they include other healthful nutrients. Supplements cannot replace a balanced diet.

Most young people who eat a balanced diet do not need to take mineral supplements.

Multivitamins come in gummy, chewable, and liquid forms that some people prefer to pills.

In general, parents should check with a doctor before giving supplements to their children. There may be medical issues to consider. For example, supplements can interact with prescription medications.

The government regulates supplements as foods, not as drugs. But supplements are regulated differently than regular foods. Anyone taking a supplement should choose a trusted source. Groups like US Pharmacopeia (USP) set quality standards for supplement makers. Also, many supplements can cause side effects. People who believe that a supplement is making them sick should stop taking it.

THINK ABOUT IT

If you take a multivitamin, it is probably a children's vitamin. Why should kids not take vitamins for adults?

TOO MANY MINERALS

It can be dangerous to take doses of minerals above recommended levels. Some minerals have a value called the tolerable upper intake level (UL). Doses above this amount can make a person very sick. Most people know that too much sodium can cause health problems. Large doses of other minerals can be harmful as well.

For children, especially, it can be possible to overdose on

Fast foods and packaged foods often contain more than the recommended daily amount of sodium.

Salt contains the important minerals sodium and chloride, but experts recommend that people restrict salt in their diet. Why could it be bad to use too much salt?

Children's multivitamins with iron are packaged to contain safe mineral dosages. Kids need less iron than adults.

trace minerals. The RDA value for these minerals is very small. For example, iron can be deadly if a child swallows too many iron supplement pills meant for adults. People who consume a lot of fortified foods or take dietary supplements should make sure that their total amounts of minerals do not exceed safe levels.

GLOSSARY

absorb To take in or swallow up.

adequate Enough for a requirement.

cell One of the tiny units that are the basic building blocks of living things.

condition A state of being, or a state in which something is wrong.

consume To eat or drink.

content An amount that is contained.

dehydration The loss of water or body fluid.

diet The food and drink that a person, animal, or group takes in.

digestion The conversion of food into simpler forms that can be used by the body.

disorder An abnormal physical or mental condition.

energy Power or ability to be active.

fortified Enriched, or having something useful added.

function The natural action of a part in a living thing.

method A way of doing something.

muscle A body tissue that can contract and produce movement.

organ A part of a person, plant, or animal that consists of cells and tissues and is specialized to do a particular task.

overdose To take too much of something (such as a drug, medicine, or vitamin).

process A continuing action or series of actions; or, to change something from one form into another by preparing or treating it in a special way.

regulate To govern or control.

restrict To place under limits as to use.

structure The arrangement or relationship of parts in a substance, body, or system.

FOR MORE INFORMATION

Books

Baggaley, Ann, Carrie Love, James Mitchem, and Fiona Hunter. *Are You What You Eat?* New York, NY: DK Publishing, 2015.

Gleisner, Jenna Lee. *My Body Needs Food.* Mankato, MN: Amicus High Interest, 2015.

Mitchem, James, and Carrie Love. *Eat Your Greens, Reds, Yellows, and Purples: Children's Cookbook.* New York, NY: DK Publishing, 2016.

Pelkki, Jane Sieving. *Healthy Eating.* New York, NY: Children's Press, 2017.

Reinke, Beth Bence, and Shahla Ray. *Nutrition Basics.* Minneapolis, MN: ABDO Publishing, 2016.

Salzmann, Mary Elizabeth. *Eat Your Vegetables! Healthy Eating Habits.* Minneapolis, MN: ABDO Publishing, 2015.

Sjonger, Rebecca. *How to Choose Foods Your Body Will Use.* New York, NY: Crabtree Publishing Company, 2016.

Websites

Arthur Family Health
http://pbskids.org/arthur/health/nutrition

Easy Science for Kids
http://easyscienceforkids.com/what-is-healthy-food-for-your-body

KidsHealth
http://kidshealth.org/en/kids/minerals.html

MedlinePlus: Minerals
https://medlineplus.gov/minerals.html

SFGate
http://healthyeating.sfgate.com/main-functions-minerals-body-4171.html

INDEX